THE SHORT AND BLOODY HISTORY OF GHOSTS

THE SHORT AND
BLOODY
HISTORY
OF
GHOSTS

John Farman

Lerner Publications Company/Minneapolis

First American edition published in 2002 by Lerner Publications Company

Copyright © 2000 by John Farman

All U.S. rights reserved. No part of this book may be reproduced, stored in a retrieval system, or transmitted in any form or by any means—electronic, mechanical, photocopying, recording, or otherwise—without the prior written permission of Lerner Publications Company, except for the inclusion of brief quotations in an acknowledged review.

This book is available in two editions:
Library binding by Lerner Publications Company, a division of Lerner Publishing Group
Soft cover by First Avenue Editions, an imprint of Lerner Publishing Group
241 First Avenue North
Minneapolis, MN 55401 U.S.A.

Website address: www.lernerbooks.com

Library of Congress Cataloging-in-Publication Data

Farman, John
    The short and bloody history of ghosts / by John Farman—1st American ed.
        p.   cm.
    Includes index.
    Summary: Presents information on the concept of ghosts throughout history and around the world, as well as famous individual "human" ghosts.
    ISBN: 0–8225–0837–0 (lib. bdg. : alk. paper)
    ISBN: 0–8225–0838–9 (pbk. : alk. paper)
    1. Ghosts—Juvenile literature. [1. Ghosts.] I. Title.
BF1461 .F37   2002
133.1'09—dc21   2001050687

Manufactured in the United States of America
1 2 3 4 5 6 – JR – 07 06 05 04 03 02

CONTENTS

How to be a Ghost   7
What are Ghosts?   9
Ghosts from around the World   13
Modern British Ghosts   24
The Spirits of London   28
British Country Ghosts   37
Ghost Stories Most Horrid   44
Inanimate Ghosts   49
Animal Ghosts   55
Nice to See You—Again   64
Things That Go Bump in the Night   73
Vampires   77
Ghost Hunting and What to Do If
    You See One   82

Ghost Speak   88
Further Reading   91
Websites   92
Index   93

HOW TO BE A GHOST

Ever wanted to be a ghost? I know it sounds kind of morbid, but I have. Think of the trouble you could get into—floating around like the Invisible Man (or Woman), getting into movies free, driving around in sports cars, or living in fancy places like Buckingham Palace. Even better, you could go around late at night scaring the wits out of people you didn't like, and, best of all, you wouldn't have to do boring things like eating, drinking, washing, or going to the bathroom. But what exactly is a ghost and what do you have to do to become one?

In simple terms, ghosts are the spirits left behind when people die. These spirits can take many forms, some invisible, some not. The one we humans seem to like most is the sort of see-through version of the person he or she or it once was.

There are many other ideas as to what ghosts really are. I suppose, if you're really considering the position, it would help to be absolutely dead, but (and I'm sorry if this disappoints you) even that doesn't necessarily guarantee ghostdom. Not everyone who dies gets to be one, you see. Actually, thank goodness for that . . . just imagine what it would be like if everyone who had ever lived was still floating around making a nuisance of themselves.

In this book, I'll try to tell you all about the best ghosts: the scariest, the weirdest, the funniest, and the nastiest.

Author's health warning: Please don't read this in a dark room all by yourself.

WHAT ARE GHOSTS?

The whole idea of dying fascinates everyone and always has. What does it actually mean? Does it just mean our money's run out and it's "game over"? Have we simply had our turn, and it's time for someone else's? Do we just turn into worm food or ashes? I'd like to think not, and so would most people.

Most religions throughout the world teach of life after death. In fact the whole of Christianity is founded on belief in the resurrection of Jesus and the presence of the Holy Spirit. People who follow gods, whether it be God, Allah, Brahma, etc., would have us believe that we've all got an immortal spirit or soul that kind of lurks around in our bodies. When our body finally gives out, this spirit usually ends up going to an allocated place like Heaven, Hell, Janna, or Jahannam. However, some souls seem to stick around, refusing to leave . . . ever, and these are the ghosts we're talking about—and in some cases, talking to.

There's a group of people who believe that they can contact and talk to ghosts whenever they feel like it. These people are called spiritualists. The ones who do the actual go-betweening are known as mediums.

Whatever we believe, the idea of being able to see beyond our death is pretty neat (even if it does scare the wits out of us at times). Throughout history, clever people like scientists, doctors, and who knows who else, have tried to tell us what ghosts really are. So what have they found out? What are ghosts made from, and why do they come back to haunt us?

Who's Who

Samuel Johnson, the famous eighteenth-century writer and clever person, was convinced that after we die, the part that makes us *us* and different from everyone else (apart from big noses and big ears), hangs around for a while refusing to stay in his or her coffin. Most times, according to Johnson, they just exist in an invisible state, and we still-alive people don't even know they're there. We only get to see the few that decide they want to be seen.

Salty Ghosts

French occult scientists right up to the twentieth century believed that when you bury someone, the salts contained in their body are released as they rot (how pleasant!). According to the occultists, when these salts escape, they begin to re-form in exactly the same position they were in before death.

So anything, from a person to a pig (or whatever), can appear to living mortals in more or less the same form—only made up of particles of salt. This is why you often see ghosts of people near graveyards and presumably ghosts of pigs near slaughterhouses (and why they're nearly always white).

These French scientists got so carried away with this idea that they even began doing experiments with blood from dead people. They set fire to the blood to see if it gave off ghostly apparitions. German occultists, on the other hand, experimented with earth dug from graveyards and claimed they saw the spirits running around in the glass vessels they used.

Unearthly Mixture

Then there are those who think that ghosts are spirits that have somehow gotten themselves entangled with a substance we can actually see. Spiritualists often refer to this as "ectoplasm," which, according to those

who know, is a lightly colored, viscous substance that actually seeps from the body of a medium (usually from the mouth). Apparently it can usually only be seen in the dark and returns to the medium's body when all the fun's over.

Ghostly Grief

Weirder still, some spiritualists believe that ghosts are the result of terrible mental strife that has imprinted memories of all of a person's previous actions and thoughts, as well as an almost photographic image, on what they call the Akasha or "astral light." It is this Akasha, allegedly, that transmits the waves of human willpower, feelings, and imagination, making it possible to be interpreted by a clairvoyant. Most scientists regard this as pure bunk.

Second Time Around

Other people reckon that we have all lived previous lives. These folks say that the ghosts we see are subconscious memories of ourselves in the clothes we once wore.

This is another form of "reincarnation," which is the term for when dead people's souls are supposed to come back to earth in other beings. (This means that, the next time around, you could still be you but living in the body of something like a hamster or jellyfish.)

Most of those who accept the idea of ghosts, however, actually believe that they really are there and are not just a figment of our imagination. These spirits, they reckon, are manufactured by the dead people themselves—some better than others, of course. Otherwise we'd be tripping over the darn things everywhere we went.

GHOSTS FROM
AROUND THE WORLD

All around the world, for as long as there've been people, there've been ghosts. Even early humans began to see things lurking in the back of the cave.★ The early people buried their dead with great respect. Who can blame them? They certainly didn't want visitors from the afterlife giving them a hard time.

JUST INVENTED

★ *Actually, there might well have been ghost monkeys as well.*

Most countries have their own ghostly traditions. Here's a sampling:

Indian Ghosts

Some of the earliest-recorded ghosts were called Bhuts and go back over a thousand years at least in Indian and Hindu mythology. The correct translation of Bhut is "has-been," which is rather appropriate when you come to think of it. Bhuts were believed to be the ghosts of people who died nastily or had not been given a proper burial. There's never been such a thing as a nice Bhut, as they have all been wicked and cruel and no fun at all.

Hot Bhuts

Bhuts live mostly in deserts, up trees, in old abandoned houses, and in the roofs of ordinary Indian people's homes. For some reason, they never—ever—touch the ground. Bhuts usually try to scare anyone they can, bhut—sorry—but, given the choice, prefer women, children, and, for some strange reason, newlyweds.

Head Bhut!

According to Hindu mythology, the boss of the Bhuts is a god called Shiva. He's pretty creepy, with three eyes, a hat made of skulls, and a huge serpent dangling around his neck. He lives high in the Himalayas with his supreme goddess girlfriend Shakti, who's also someone you wouldn't want to meet in a dark alley. I suppose their extreme grumpiness is almost understandable, for one of their sons, Skanda, was born with six heads and the other, Ganesha, was given the head of an elephant. (Imagine what they must have had to put up with at ghost school.)

Ghost Curry

There were also believed to be other ghosts in India called Bautas. These were horrid little guys with small red bodies and big heads with fangs like lions. They came out mostly at night and gibbered in a high nasal tone. In order to stay on their good

OH NO – NOT CURRY AGAIN

side, the peasants would build tall piles of stones on top of which they would leave freshly prepared food (probably the very first take-out food).

Assyrian Ghosts

Assyria was the kingdom in northern Mesopotamia that became the center of one of the greatest empires of the ancient Middle East. It dates from the fourteenth to the sixth century B.C. The Assyrians believed in a horrid type of ghost called an alû, who used to terrify the natives. It hung out in caves, ruins, and abandoned buildings and was described as "horrible in appearance—half human and sometimes without a mouth, ears, or limbs." Personally, I couldn't see what harm a person with all those things missing could do to you (rub you to death?). That was until I read that your average alû could envelop his victim like a cloak and squeeze the living daylights out of him.

Ghosts Egyptian Style

The ancient Egyptians believed in more ghosts and demons than you could shake a mummy at. These ghosts apparently glided over the land trying to harm anyone they met. In ancient days, Egyptians thought that man consisted of a physical body, a spiritual body, a shadow, a soul, a heart, and—and this is where the trouble started—a spirit called khu.

Now each khu, so the story goes, felt terribly lonely when its person died and so went around causing healthy people to fall ill out of spite. It was also fond of getting right inside animals' heads and making them go crazy. Ordinary people's khus were bad enough, but the khus of people who'd killed themselves, been criminals, or were unburied were absolutely horrible and not to be messed with at all.

Ghost Alarm

Egyptian ghosts were good at attacking visitors, especially those trying to steal stuff from the tombs of their ancient pharaohs. In March 1971, Professor Walter Emery, age sixty-seven, suffered a massive stroke in Cairo just after he'd unearthed a statue of Osiris, the Egyptian god. Unfortunately for old Walt, Osiris turned out to be the god of death. Worse luck still, Walt had actually been searching for Imhotep, the god of medicine, who presumably could have made him better.

Leave Mummy Alone

Finding ancient mummies is a dangerous business. More than twenty-six people connected with the discovery of the tomb of Tutankhamen in 1923 came to sudden and sometimes violent ends, including Lord George Carnarvon, the leader of the expedition, who'd been warned several times by mystics and seers. He died of an infected mosquito bite.

WARNING!!!!

Just in case you're ever tempted to go a-mummying yourself, read this cautionary tale. Decide for yourself whether you believe it or not.

In the late nineteenth century, a Cairo merchant offered a young man called Douglas Murray and his two friends the highly ornate and priceless mummy case of a beautiful young girl.

Murray bought the exquisite antiquity but a few days later was badly injured in a duck-shooting accident that caused him to lose his right arm. (The duck, by the way, was fine, you'll be pleased to know.) On the journey back to England, his two companions fell ill from some foreign bug and had to be dumped overboard—sorry—buried at sea. So far so bad.

When Murray finally got home to London, he found the mummy case waiting for him. But the painted face of the pretty young girl now seemed old and mean. He took the case to be photographed at a nearby studio. It was the last snap shot the photographer ever took—he died shortly afterward from a mystery illness (mummylaria?).

A female journalist then came by to take the mummy away and have it examined, as part of a long piece she was writing about Douglas Murray. As soon as she got the thing home, however, her mother fell down the stairs stone dead, her two champion dogs went mad, and her fiancé, rather sensibly I think, ended their engagement. She, in turn, became very ill and couldn't wait to give the darn thing back to Murray. He, realizing it was a bit of a liability to say the least, quickly donated it to the British Museum, which was delighted.

The carrier, who was given the job of delivering the cursed thing, died a week later, as did the man employed to study the hieroglyphics on the case. The poor guy apparently died of exhaustion having not slept a wink since he'd first laid eyes on the mummy. But it gets worse. The press photographer, who had taken a picture of the case as it arrived at the museum, was shocked as he developed the picture. Instead of the pretty young girl he'd seen in the camera, he witnessed the face of a woman so hideous that he went into the other room and promptly blew his brains out. Now that's ugly!

The museum authorities removed the mummy from public exhibition after guards reported sobbing coming from the empty case. The museum cleaners revolted and refused to go near it. The British Museum then decided to give it to a museum in New York.

Three guesses which famous ship they sent it out on? You're right, they chose the maiden voyage of the *Titanic*. In 1912 the ship hit an iceberg, and the mummy case sank to the bottom and was, thank God, never heard of again. Unfortunately nor were the 1,500 passengers who went down with it.

Moral of the story: Never buy anything off a stranger in Cairo.

Ghosts Arab Style

If a person was murdered in an Arab country, the person's afreet or specter would supposedly pop up from the ground where it had happened. The only way to get over this problem, so they say, was to hammer a large new nail into the ground at the scene of the crime. This apparently pinned the specter to the ground before it could get into any mischief. This could be where the old driving-a-nail-into-a-vampire-to-kill-him idea came from. Dating afreets precisely is tricky, but they crop up in the ancient scriptures of Islam and are still believed in today.

Ghosts Abroad

Here's a weird story about a ghost who traveled all the way from the Holy Land to England in the thirteenth century. William Longespee was brutally hacked to pieces by Arab fighters during the Crusades. At the exact moment of his death (as it later turned out), the specter of a knight appeared to his mother, the Abbess of Lacock, in Wiltshire. The poor

spirit looked skeletal, so much so that even his own mother didn't recognize him. Till he spoke . . .

"I am your son William, and I have been brought down to honor God's name." Just to prove it, he showed his mother his own personal insignia painted in ghost paint on his ghost shield. None of the abbess's friends believed her until six months later. At that time, official reports of the time of her son's death arrived back in England. They matched the very same day and hour that she saw his spirit.

The Spirited Romans

Life in ancient Rome was riddled with ghosts. You might have heard about their greatest emperor Julius Caesar, whose ghost came back to haunt his assassin Brutus (one of his generals). There are thousands of other Roman ghost stories. Here is one that was recorded by Pliny, the famous writer.

The story goes that there was a house haunted by a male ghost who dragged a heavy ghost-chain behind him, making an awful noise and frightening men, women, and pets alike. Athenodouros, a famous philosopher, rented the house, thinking he was clever enough to quiet the ghost down. On the first night, the noisy ghost turned up as usual in the study where the philosopher was philosophizing. Athenodouros thought he'd fool him by taking no notice, but eventually the loud clinking noise got on his nerves. When he turned around, the ghost beckoned Athenodouros to follow him to the courtyard where it pointed to a particular spot on the ground and then vanished.

The following morning, after a good night's sleep, the philosopher took his shovel and started digging at the spot. There he found the skeleton of a man bound in chains. Athenodouros then had the corpse publicly burned, and the ghost was never seen again.

Chinless Chinese Ghosts

Just about every ancient Chinese person had a complete terror of ghosts—especially those of ex-murderers. They appeared, so the ancient books say, in a most peculiar way— first the head, then the feet, then the rest. The only parts that didn't appear were their chins.

The Chinese did everything to try to keep on the good side of their chinless ghosts. They'd pin money and pictures of their best warriors to the walls and perform ceremonies like the "Appeasing of the Burning Mouths,"* where they put plates of cakes out with invitations to the "Honorable Homeless Ghosts."

Hair Scare

In May 1876, complete panic broke out in the streets of Nanking (modern Nanjing). Invisible demons were running around cutting off everyone's pigtails. For ages afterward, men and women walked around clutching their hair for safety. The panic spread to Shanghai, but by this time the ghosts had turned to crushing sleeping people to death, which was a lot more serious. This hair cutting and body crushing went on for over three years. Way nasty.

IT WASN'T ME - HONEST

* *You'd have thought this ceremony would have been for those Indian curry-eating ghosts.*

Japanese Ghosts

Old Japanese spirits, particularly from the 1100s to the 1300s, were very odd. There were women ghosts with bad haircuts wearing long white robes and legless Samurai warrior-ghosts. There were foxes that could change into beautiful women and then bewitch anyone who crossed their path.

Caribbean Ghosts

If you're going to be a ghost anywhere, might I suggest the warm and sunny islands of the Caribbean? Many weird and wonderful cults came over to the Caribbean from West Africa via the slave trade in the eighteenth century. Most notable are Obeah in Jamaica and voodoo in Haiti. Both cults have been connected with witchcraft and black magic, but voodoo actually mentions an ancient supreme being. These cults are, in fact, very close to spiritualism, being merely a more dramatic way of calling back the spirits of their dead ancestors, as well as Loa, the spirits of African gods and old Catholic saints.

The way they do it is quite simple. A group of drummers slowly builds up a rhythm while those who would like to be possessed by the spirits of the dead prance around. Usually some poor animal, like a goat or a chicken, gets its throat cut for good measure. As the pace of the drumming increases to fever pitch, the dancer goes into a sort of a trance. This is the signal for the spirit or Loa to enter.

Many of the spirits are nice and well meaning, but apparently a zombie sometimes turns up, which is not such good news. Zombies are supposed to be either the disembodied souls of dead people or the actual corpses themselves that have popped up out of the ground for the party.

MODERN BRITISH GHOSTS

In the olden days, ghosts drifted around drafty old castles and stuff. These days they've got a whole lot of nice shiny machinery to play with. Here are a few examples of the tricks they pull.

Happy Photos

In 1975 a photo was published of the squadron of Sir Victor Goddard, a retired officer in Britain's Royal Air Force (RAF). The photo showed a group of officers from World War I. The strange thing about the photo was that it included the face of air mechanic Freddie Jackson peeping over his friend's shoulder. Strange, because earlier Freddie had been at his own funeral on the very day the photo was taken—he'd been banged fatally on the head by a propeller (with the plane switched on).

Ghost Bus-ters

There have been a lot of fatal accidents at a particular corner bus stop in London, England. At the point where Saint Marks Road joins Cambridge Gardens, there had been reports of a strange driverless bus, with lights ablaze, running long after all the other buses were safely in their bus garage.

Following one particularly gruesome accident, the inquest heard from dozens of London residents who'd sighted the runaway bus. Some even said they'd waited for all the tire screeching to be over before they could get to sleep. In the end, the local government moved the bus stop, and the phantom bus was never seen again. One is tempted to ask how all the other ghosts got home after that.

Ghosts on TV

In 1993 a family in London decided to take photos of themselves while they were all together at Christmas. When the pictures were developed, there appeared to be a strange woman's face on the television in the background. So what, I hear you say.

The trouble was—the TV had been switched off all day. When the press got hold of the strange story and published the pictures in the papers, several people commented that the woman looked just like Doris Stokes, a famous medium. Stranger still, the poor old dear had been dead for several years. Time for a new television, I'd have thought.

Ghost Rock

Here's another story from 1993. A family in Falkirk, Scotland, reported that every night at the same time their son's toy guitar played ghostly music when there was no one near it. Paranormal investigators were called in, and sure enough at a given time it began to play. The guitar was duly taken away to be tested, but the darn thing refused to perform anywhere else (temperamental or what!). Weirder than that, the music continued after it was gone.

In desperation, the researchers went through a cupboard near where the guitar had stood. Behind a whole bunch of household junk was a musical toy that was setting itself off at the same time every night.

Ha Ha! Let that be a lesson to you. Don't believe everything people tell you.

Ghosts Go Clubbing

At the end of the 1990s, the alarm went off at a British police station indicating a break-in at Butterflies, a local night club. The police rushed to the site and found that nothing appeared to have been disturbed. Just to make sure, they ran the security videotape. Imagine their surprise when they saw a man walking along the corridor as clear as day and then through the door at the end. Neither the manager nor his staff had ever laid eyes on him before. Strange, but even stranger when you consider the guy hadn't opened the door first.

THE SPIRITS OF LONDON

All cities have their ghosts, but London seems to have more than its fair share. If you ever come to visit, why not try and find these places and scare yourself witless?

Meat off the Bone

London's Smithfield meat market goes back many centuries. In 1654 butchers began to complain about the ghost of a well-known local lawyer called Mallet. On Saturday nights between nine and twelve, he'd drift between the market stalls, throwing around all the joints of meat. Despite the angry butchers lunging at him with their knives and cleavers, they only managed to endanger each other. Pictures of him show that he wore extremely long pointy shoes by the way.

But that's not all—by far. Way back in history, Smithfield was called Smoothfield and was the site for hundreds of executions. Most famous was that of Roose, the cook of the bishop of Rochester. He was executed in 1530 for poisoning the soup of the bishop's household, killing two and causing another seventeen to be very ill.

The method of his death was most appropriate. He was tied up and

NO SECONDS!

lowered into a huge cauldron of boiling water, which presumably made soup of him, too. The poor ex-cook has also been seen (pre-cooked and ladle in hand) walking the streets of Smithfield.

During the reign of Queen Mary I, in the sixteenth century, 270 Protestants were burned to death immediately opposite the Church of Saint Bartholomew the Great (which is still there). In 1849 work crews excavating a sewer on the site found a layer of ashes and human bones just three feet below the ground. In case there was any doubt as to their identity, they also dug up oak posts, together with chains and rings that the victims had been attached to. Needless to say, every now and again the occasional bloodcurdling shriek and the sounds of wood burning can be heard.

Riding Forbidden

Some ghosts have no regard for public laws. Jerry Abershaw, a famous eighteenth-century highwayman (robber), gallops his horse at full speed across Wimbledon Common regularly, despite signs prohibiting horse riding between sunset and sunrise. I suppose if I'd been hung in 1795, I wouldn't care about rules and regulations either.

Shot in the Dark

A woman was walking through a graveyard in Hammersmith in 1804. All of a sudden, a white phantom, which had been seen a little earlier by some other people passing in a carriage, chased her between the gravestones. She died a little later from the shock.

Patrols of men went out for several nights to try to get to the bottom of the mystery. On the fourth night, sure enough, a figure in white was seen crossing the graveyard. Francis Smith, a customs officer, shot at the figure, but instead of the bullet passing straight through, as it should have, the figure fell to the ground. No wonder—it turned out to be painter and decorator Thomas Milwood, still in his white decorating clothes, staggering home late from the pub. Whoops!

THAT AIN
NO GHOS

The Bloody Ghost of Saint James Palace

If you really don't like ghosts, then don't go near Henry VIII's palace built in 1532 at Saint James (and stop reading this book!). It is supposed to be one of the most haunted places in Britain. Here is just one of a hundred stories.

In the part of the palace that looks sort of like a country estate, the body of a man propped up in a bed drenched in blood has been seen many times. The story goes like this. Ernest, the duke of Cumberland, came home one night in 1810, after attending the opera and then misbehaving in Covent Garden. He then, apparently, murdered his Italian servant called Sellis by holding his hair and practically severing his head with a sword.

In court, the duke said that it was self-defense and that Sellis had attacked him for no reason. Then the servant had just gone to bed and slit his own throat (very likely, your Lordship).

It turned out the old duke had had his wicked way with the poor servant's pretty daughter, who, finding herself pregnant, committed suicide rather than face the disgrace. The duke then killed her father to shut him up. Like all aristocracy in those days, the duke literally got away with murder but was booed in the streets for the rest of his miserable life.

Every now and again, even to this day, scuffling sounds can be heard in the room accompanied by the sickening smell of freshly spilled blood.

The Black Nun

Here's a sad one. For 200 years until 1973 the vaults of the Bank of England were patrolled to protect the country's gold. But apparently they weren't the only ones walking the dingy corridors. The so-called black nun, Sarah Whitehead, still does to this day—not to protect the gold but to find her long lost brother.

Philip Whitehead, a Bank of England clerk, was arrested in 1811 and charged with forgery. He was later hung for the crime, which made his loving sister lose her mind. The following day she was back at the bank dressed in black from head to foot and wearing a thick veil. For over twenty-five years, she walked up and down Threadneedle Street (where the bank is) asking person after person if they'd seen her poor brother.

But her death didn't end it there. Sarah was buried in a graveyard that later became the bank's formal gardens. Bank clerks at the turn of the century began to see the poor woman regularly, sobbing and pounding her gravestone with her fists.

MORNING!

Jack's Back

Two of Jack the Ripper's most famous victims have been seen again in London. His first victim in 1888, Polly Nichols, was originally found with her throat slashed and her stomach cut open. Ever since, passersby on Durward Street have spotted a stooped figure glowing eerily in the gutter. Another of his victims, Annie Chapman, is sometimes still heard screaming on Hansbury Street.

Terry, the Ghost of the Subway

Ghosts turn up in the most unlikely places with unlikely names, but none is more odd than Terry the Ghost of Covent Garden Station. Like most of the older subway stations, Covent Garden is a rabbit warren of dark corridors and staircases. Until very recently, there have been reports of a strange guy in old-fashioned clothes and pale leather gloves drifting around the station. Railway workers hate working there, because they often hear strange gasps and sighs, echoey footsteps, loud banging, and even the occasional muted scream. All normal subway stuff, right? Maybe not, when you consider that they've all been heard well after the trains have stopped running.

CAN I SEE YOUR TICKET?

TICKETS

In the late 1950s, a clairvoyant was sent to Covent Garden to see if he could sort it out. He saw the ghost almost immediately and said that it was trying to give him a name that sounded like Terry. Local historians showed him a picture of William Terris, an actor-manager who'd died a long time ago in suspicious circumstances, and the clairvoyant was positive it was him.

The highly successful Terris had been stabbed in 1897 as he was leaving the Adelphi Theatre (which is still there). As he was dying, he just managed to tell everyone that he'd be back—which was very nice of him. His murderer, Richard Prince, a jealous actor, was found nearby, screaming and foaming at the mouth.

Since then, Terris has been seen all over the place—in the theater, in the street, but most of all in the tunnels in and around Covent Garden Station.

Ghostly Stabbing

Not all ghosts are harmless. In April 1922, there was a report of a man who was happily strolling down Coventry Street, when he turned into an alley and thought he heard footsteps behind him. He turned around, but there was no one to be seen. Suddenly he felt himself being stabbed in the neck. When he was found and rushed to a London hospital, the doctors were sure he'd been attacked by somebody, even though he hadn't seen any assailant. That was until another man, and then another, turned up with exactly the same wound from exactly the same location with exactly the same story. Scary!!

The Ghost Streaker

If you like ghosts of tall old men with no clothes on, I might be able to help you (somebody should!). Get yourself down to Cleopatra's Needle, that strange, granite obelisk by the Thames River. There you'll see the shadowy figure of a man, as naked as the day he was born, running along the wall and then diving into the river without a splash. All that is heard is a scary moaning sound and mocking laughter. I'd have thought you'd have heard the chattering of teeth, too.

Ghosts at the BBC

The huge British Broadcasting Corporation (BBC) building in Langham Place is haunted. On the second and third floors, many people claim to have seen the ghost of an ancient butler, walking in slow motion with an empty tray. In one particular room, others have witnessed a large batlike creature jumping out of a wall.

The Creepy Tree of Death

I've been told that there's a strange tree in Green Park, in which no birds ever settle, under which no drunks ever drink, near which no children ever play. Many people have apparently hung themselves from its gruesomely twisted branches over the years. The tall figure of a man has often been seen nearby but is said to disappear whenever a second glance is attempted. Park attendants swear that sometimes when they are passing they hear strange noises, like the clashing of swords or horrible evil laughter or the occasional agonized groan. This tree had been the scene of various duels and murders going right back to the eighteenth century. I don't know about you, but I can't wait to find it.

BRITISH COUNTRY GHOSTS

I always prefer to think of ghosts living in deserted rural areas, rather than big cities. Here are a few of the strangest ghost stories from the countryside around Britain.

The Weaver Who Wouldn't Play Dead

There's a little village called Deane Combe in southwestern England where a very successful weaver called Knowles once lived. When he died, he was duly buried. But when his son arrived to take over the business the following morning, he was surprised to find his old man still there, sitting where he'd always sat, weaving away to his heart's content. The son went to get the local parson. He, in turn, heard the weaver's shuttle from the bottom of the stairs leading to the workroom and called the spirit down. The parson reminded the ghostly Knowles, in no uncertain terms, that he was dead and had no business being there. The old dead weaver apologized but said he'd gone and died halfway through a job and had to finish it. The parson, expecting this reply, had brought a handful of earth from the graveyard and promptly threw it into the poor ghost's face. Suddenly the dead weaver turned into a large black dog. The vicar beckoned it to follow him and together they walked through a small wood to a lake below a waterfall. He then gave the dog half a walnut shell and ordered him to empty the lake with it and not rest until he had finished.

To this day it is said that the dog can be seen either at midday or midnight laboriously emptying the lake one shellful at a time.

The Hairy Hands

Here a story from Dartmoor. This bleak wilderness lies in southwestern England and has been the location of a convict prison since 1850.

There's a lonely road that crosses Dartmoor between Moretonhampstead and Two Bridges. One day in June 1921, the medical officer to Dartmoor Prison was riding this road on his motorcycle, with his two children in the sidecar. According to the children, just as they were approaching the bridge that crosses the Dart River, the doctor suddenly yelled, "There's something wrong, jump for it!"

The next moment the motorcycle swerved. The doctor left the seat and landed yards away . . . on his head—dead. The two children were luckily unhurt.

A month or so later, a young army officer was also motorcycling on the same piece of road when he, too, was thrown from the seat. He was only knocked out, however, and when able to speak claimed that a pair of hairy hands closed over his hands and drove him off the road.

Since then, there have been several reports of old "hairy hands" getting into mischief. Scarier still is the fact that I found a reference in a book to the ghostly hands on that very same lonely moorland road between Two Bridges and Postbridge, going way back before cars or motorcycles were invented.

The Perils of Alcohol

There's a little pub in Norton St. Philip, Somerset, called the Fleur de Lys. The building opposite it used to be the courthouse and over 300 years ago a bunch of rebels were tried there. When they were found guilty, they were dragged across the road to the orchard behind the Fleur de Lys to be hung.

One poor customer held open the gate for the miserable wretches as they went to their doom. The stupid soldiers accompanying them mistook him for one of the prisoners and promptly strung him up, too.

In 1974 William Harris, who owned the pub, heard chains being dragged, and his wife saw a ghostly figure actually walking into the bar.

Glamis★ Castle

If you want to be guaranteed a sighting of a ghost, you could do far worse than get yourself invited to Glamis Castle, Macbeth's old place in Scotland. They've got more than ten ghosts in constant residence who are still, apparently, opening and shutting doors and making a huge nuisance of themselves.

Glamis Castle is supposed to have been home to the "Monster of Glamis," who was born in 1800. This poor kid was so ugly, so they say, that they had to shut him away so that no one could see him. (So what—we did that with my brother!)

Among the other old faithfuls is the "Gray Lady," who always hangs around the chapel and "Earl Beardie," who lost his soul to the devil in a card game in one of the towers and was doomed to play cards forever. Lady Glamis always hovers above the clock tower, so she must be useful if you need to know the time. There's also a tall figure in a cloak, a bunch of characters inhabiting the Blue Room, and a small woman who can sometimes be seen looking anxiously out of an upstairs window. If you look outside, you can see a tongueless woman who's continually trotting (quietly) backward and forward across the park and "Jack the Runner," a man who only runs on the castle driveway. A madman (with a great sense of balance) walks across the roof on stormy nights.

With that big group, I'm surprised there's any room for *real* people.

★*(pronounced "glarms")*

Ghostly Sing-Along

Derelict or deserted castles and stately homes have always been homes for ghosts. You've only got to see Ewloe Castle in Clwyd, Wales, and you'll feel a shiver down your spine. Quite recently the present owner not only heard ghostly singing but saw a phantom shape pass right through a hedge. His poor dog was so terrified that it went into a decline and died a couple of days later. The vet could find absolutely nothing wrong with him (apart from being dead).

Similarly, at Hardwick Hall, in central England, two little girls in 1934 claimed they saw a ghost playing in the ruins. He looked real enough apparently, but the fact that he was floating around on the level where the second floor had been gave the game away. One of the girls, Winifred Chambers, remembered it vividly even when grown up. He apparently had a florid smiling face, with high buckled shoes, riding pants, an open shirt, and an apron. He was carrying a tray of drinks (a dangerous business with no floor). She took him to be an old-fashioned servant.

Monkey Business

Monks and nuns are often reported in ghostly form. In eastern England in the late 1970s, a ghostly monk appeared to motorists around Christmas time. Local police, always guaranteed to be somewhat skeptical, claimed it was a well-known local tramp, but unless the old boy had borrowed a monk's cowl and learned to float a few feet in the air, it couldn't have been.

Smoking Spooks

Throughout the highways and byways of Britain, phantom hitchhikers have been common. In 1951 a security police officer was driving around the Lakenheath Royal Air Base in Suffolk. In his headlights, he saw an RAF pilot in uniform flagging him down. He stopped to give him a lift. The hitchhiker had only been in the car a couple of minutes when he asked the driver for a cigarette, which he gave him. The driver then handed him his lighter and watched out of the corner of his eye as the pilot lit the cigarette. When he stopped at a checkpoint, he turned to his new companion, only to find there was no one there. But the lighter was lying on the seat, and a faint whiff of tobacco smoke filled the car.

GHOST STORIES
MOST HORRID

Quite a lot of ghost stories are minor affairs. You know the sort of thing—pale ladies in long floating dresses, gliding up the stairs or drifting through graveyards. But others are really nasty.

The Curse of the Gallows

There's a tiny speck of land, called Norfolk Island in the middle of the Pacific Ocean 900 miles east of Australia. It was used as a prison by the British until the end of the nineteenth century. There are only a few people living there now, but most of those have reported seeing the ghosts of dead convicts who were hung there. From this grim place comes the tale of Barney Duffy's curse.

GONE TO LUNCH

Barney Duffy was a huge Irish convict who escaped from the jail and was found by two soldiers hiding out in a hollow tree. The penalty for escaping was death by hanging. Duffy warned the soldiers, "If you take me back to that dreadful place, you will die violently within a week of my hanging."

They ignored his wild threat, and poor old Duffy swung from the gallows as soon as he got back. End of story? Two days later, the two soldiers went fishing near the spot where they had found the convict hiding. The next morning, their torn and mutilated bodies were found lying at the water's edge. And it wasn't fish, seagulls, or mermaids that had done it.

The Bad Teacher Alert

Ever since Dame Elizabeth Hoby died in 1609, her ghost has been seen wandering around her old home, Bisham Abbey in central England. Poor Elizabeth, who was a close friend of Queen Elizabeth I, died in misery for something she had done earlier in her life.

It all started with her youngest boy William, who was by all accounts kind of a dunce at his schoolwork. In those days, before good schools were invented, kids were often taught by their parents or governesses. Anyway, William's attempts at writing and penmanship were really bad. Although his mother would beat him with great regularity (the view being that this would help him focus his efforts), the beatings never seemed to do any good.

One day his spelling was worse than ever and covered in errors and ink blots. His mother lost control completely, beating him soundly and locking him in a cupboard to teach him the lesson he'd obviously ignored. Suddenly a message came from Queen Elizabeth, saying that Dame Hoby was needed at court right away. I bet you can guess where this is going.

When she got back late that night, Dame Hoby felt sorry for her terrible temper attack earlier and went to little Will's room to apologize. He wasn't there of course. She suddenly remembered that she'd locked him in the cupboard. When she got there, however, the poor kid was dead, slumped over a pile of books. In those days, there were no child-welfare agencies so Elizabeth Hoby got away with it.

Her ghost has mostly been seen drifting through the abbey grounds, wringing her hands in front of her. But in 1840, work crews doing repairs found several books with children's writing in them that had slipped down beneath the floorboards under a cupboard. One of the pages was almost unreadable. It looked as if it had been drenched in tears. Let that be a lesson to all of you who don't do your homework neatly.

Horrible Hands

Way back in the 1790s, a woman traveler arrived at the old Spital Inn on a lonely moor in Ireland. She asked to be allowed to sit in front of the fire for a while before continuing her journey. The landlord asked a maid to sit with her, but the maid thought it strange when she saw men's pants peeping out just below the traveler's long skirts. As soon as the maid appeared to be asleep, so the story goes, the traveler brought out a dismembered hand that had a candle wedged between its fingers. The hand belonged to an executed criminal. The man, for indeed the traveler was a man, then said, "Let all who sleep, sleep on, let those who are awake be awake." He then went to try to open the locked door to let his friends in.

The maid, who had only been pretending to be asleep, rushed upstairs to warn the landlord that the door was being broken down. He wouldn't wake up, just as the legend promised. She remembered the old tale that said that this particular type of candle (which was still burning on the table downstairs) could only be put out with milk. The maid dashed to the kitchen and tipped a whole jug over the hand.

The landlord and his staff woke instantly and heard the commotion downstairs. The robbers left with nothing apart from a bunch of shotgun pellets in their backsides.

By the way, the candle holder was known as the Hand of Glory, and the actual candle had to be made from fat from the hanged man's flesh, virgin wax, and something called Lapland sesame oil, should you want to make one.

The Bell Witch

In the eighteenth century in Tennessee, John Bell, a rich plantation owner and friend of President Andrew Jackson, was plagued by an unpleasant ghost in his huge plantation house. He called in an investigator called William Porter, who agreed to sleep over.

On the very first night, Porter had the alarming experience of having a ghost jump into his bed, roll up the bedclothes into a tight ball, and give off the foulest smell imaginable. Porter was, as you can imagine, darned annoyed. He grabbed the ball of smelly bedclothes with the idea of throwing them out but found them so heavy that he couldn't even lift them. Eventually, the stink was so bad that Porter had to rush into the cold night air to get away from it.

Following this, between the years of 1771 and 1821, one of the children in the Bell household began throwing up pins and needles, which is all right if you have a load of sewing to do, but otherwise . . .

John Bell died mysteriously in 1821 from poisoning, and soon after a huge glowing ball came out of his chimney, blew apart, and a loud voice was heard to say, "I'm going to be gone for seven years." Everyone presumed it was the ghost and was naturally happy to hear it. Nobody seems to know if the ghost kept his word.

INANIMATE GHOSTS

Most people think ghosts are only see-through versions of dead people. Throughout history, however, lots of different things have come back to haunt us.

Home Is Where the Head Is

Body parts are always good in haunting circles, but none is better than the human skull. Theophilus Brome's skull is a good example. Theophilus, a farmer from western England, fought during the English Civil War in the seventeenth century. He sided with the king at first but later went over to the rebels because he couldn't bear what the royal side was doing to its prisoners—chopping off their heads, then shoving them on spikes and waving them around as trophies. When, in 1670, he was about to die, he asked his sister if it wasn't too much trouble to have his head taken from his body so no one could do the same to him. He also asked that it never leave the house where he'd lived his whole life.

Since that time, many of the people who took over Brome's old farm have attempted to get rid of the dratted thing only to be scared silly by the sound of horrid screaming. One person was so upset that he decided to put the skull back in the grave with the rest of Theophilus. When the shovel snapped in half while digging up the grave, it seemed pretty clear that this might not be the best idea in the world.

I DID WARN YOU

The digger stopped and took the skull home again. lt still lives happily in Higher Chilton Farm and has actually brought good luck to many of the subsequent inhabitants.

Having said that, on one occasion in the 1970s, Dave Allen, the Irish comedian, visited the farm to do a show. He was apparently so scared by something that happened on the way home that he swore he'd never go near the place again, friendly skull or no friendly skull.

Spooky Bristol

For some obscure reason, the city of Bristol in western England can often be seen floating in the sky over Alaska between June 21 and July 10. Why Bristol? Nobody knows. It was first reported by the indigenous Alaskans way before the first white settlers arrived. In 1887 a famous pioneer, William Willoughby, was so amazed by the apparition that he decided to take its photo. Despite his protestations, hardly anyone could believe that it wasn't just a picture of—er—Bristol. Since then, many ghost cities have been seen in the Alaskan skies, but most of them are said to look like ancient cities from the past. (I bet you think I'm making this up.)

Ghost Ships

The chief of the Campbell clan, the duke of Argyll, still has the picture of a strange galley, complete with sails and oars, on his coat of arms. Legend has it that when any prominent member of the family dies, the ship appears on Loch Fyne in Scotland.

In 1913 the ship was seen by hundreds of people at the death of Lord Archibald Campbell, sailing across the loch with its usual crew of three seamen. When it reached the loch's shore, it continued overland to the sanctuary of Saint Colomba, the Irish priest who brought Christianity to Scotland.

The Flying Dutchman

Despite the pleading of his crew, a nineteenth-century Dutch captain called Hendrik van der Decken attempted to sail his ship in a terrible storm around the Cape of Good Hope, in southern Africa. The ship went down like a stone, but legend has it that the silly captain was condemned to sail the seas for all of eternity in his ghostly ship while luring other ships to the same fate.

The most convincing sighting was in 1939, when more than one hundred people saw the ship, in full sail, passing Glencairn Beach in False Bay, near Cape Town, South Africa. There was not a breath of wind that day.

The most famous witness was Prince George, who later became King George V. He and many others saw the vessel on the night of July 11, 1881, off the southern coast of Australia. He said it gave off an eerie light that lit up all its masts and sails. Although the officer of the watch and the quarterdeck midshipman also saw the ship, when they all ran up to the front of the boat to get a better view, the vessel had disappeared without a trace. It was a clear, calm night.

I don't want to pour cold water on their story, but I recently read that there's an atmospheric condition called Saint Elmo's Fire that causes the ends of masts on sailing ships to glow with an eerie, greenish light.

Now You See It, Now You Don't

In the 1930s, a young girl called Edna Hodges was bicycling along to visit her friend. A storm blew up, and it started to rain. The little girl, frightened of the thunder, decided to ask for shelter at an isolated little thatched cottage that looked warm and welcoming.

She was met at the door by a tall man with a gray beard, who beckoned her to come in. Oddly enough, when she got inside the cozy cottage, all sounds of the raging storm disappeared. The old man smiled but never spoke (he sounds more dangerous than the storm). Suddenly, young Edna found herself back on the road on her bike, continuing on her journey, having no memory of actually leaving the cottage.

When she turned up at her friend's house, the girl's parents, who'd been worried about her getting soaked, were mystified that she was perfectly dry. She explained what had happened but was told that the only house along that stretch of road was completely derelict and hadn't been occupied for years and years. I think I'd rather have gotten soaked—how about you?

The Blank Check

On November 28, 1931, Ina Jephson received a letter from her lawyer containing a hefty check. She couldn't get to the bank that day, so she carried the check around in her bag, looking at it occasionally to make sure it was still there. When she got home, she looked again, but this time it was gone. She searched high and low for the thing but in the end had to write to the lawyer to tell him she'd lost the check and ask him to stop the payment.

How could he, he replied in the following letter, he hadn't sent it yet. He enclosed the real check, which, according to Miss Jephson, was identical to the first "ghost" one.

The Plane Truth

Sir Michael Bruce, a former RAF pilot, was sent on a training course in southern England in 1944. Part of the instruction involved finding good sites for gun emplacements. Five senior officers and the young Bruce drove off in a jeep to mark one of these sites.

They were traveling along the road that passes Stonehenge when they all saw a small aircraft that appeared to be in trouble. They watched it fly lower and lower and then dive headlong into a clump of trees. The men raced to see if they could save the pilot but found nothing when they got there. Suddenly one of them called the others over to a stone marker. His face was ghostly white as he read that it had been built as a memorial to the very first death from a plane crash in England in 1912. Phew!

ANIMAL GHOSTS

If your dog, cat, or even bunny rabbit dies, fear not, you might well see them again. Animals make good ghosts as the next few examples will suggest.

The Ghost Bear

There's a house in a fashionable part of London that was supposed to have been built on the site of an old bear-baiting ring. Tormenting bears was all the rage in the seventeenth century. All over London there were special arenas where the poor things were blinded and then torn to pieces by specially bred mastiffs—for fun! A particular phantom bear has been seen by several occupants stumbling around the garden in a frenzy (that's the bear, not the occupants).

Of course, that's nothing—another person of the same house was known to rush from the living room every time she saw the vision of a woman lying on the sofa with her throat cut. The house had been the scene of a particularly brutal murder long ago.

Beware—Frozen Chicken Alert!

Be warned. If for any reason you venture anywhere near London's Pond Square, you might be in for a big surprise. A frightful phantom chicken has been seen many times, as naked as the day it came out of its egg, shivering, squawking at the top of its beak, and running around in ever-decreasing circles. It actually happens to be one of the most famous hens in history.

In 1626 Sir Francis Bacon—the famous politician, writer, and scientist—was traveling home in his coach one snowy winter's day when he noticed that the snow removed by the carriage wheels revealed fresh green grass despite the ground having been covered for weeks (strange guy!). Aha!—he thought—if snow can preserve grass, perhaps it can preserve other things. So saying, he ordered his coachman to go and buy a chicken from the farm up the road (as you would), then throttle it, pluck it, and fill the poor clucker with snow. He then got him to put the hapless hen in a bag and stuffed more snow around it.

It was, as we now know, the very first frozen chicken. Unfortunately Sir Francis wasn't around to witness his momentous discovery. The silly guy caught a cold while the experiment was being carried out and died of pneumonia only a couple of days later.

Oddly enough, Sir Francis Bacon himself has never been seen in ghostly form . . . but that darned chicken has! She's been seen over twenty times in the twentieth century alone. The last sighting was in 1970 when a couple, who were kissing on a doorstep in Pond Square, were surprised when a big, white, naked bird dropped to the ground in front of them (some people have all the luck). It was the chicken, in case you're wondering, and after flapping about for a few seconds, it disappeared into thin air.

Hellhounds

The most common four-legged phantoms are usually known as hellhounds and take the form of huge black dogs. Most deserted regions have them.

The most popular (if you can use that word) hellhound is called the Black Shuck, and he prowls around the lonely fenlands of eastern England, finding his way around by the light from his huge, single red eye.

During World War II, a young American airman and his wife were renting a small house on the edge of the Walberswick Marshes near the airbase where he served. One fearful night, there was a dreadful pounding on the door. Looking through the window, the young man saw it was the dreaded Black Shuck. He'd only heard about it a few days before and was scared out of his wits. The terrified couple piled what furniture they had against the door, while the hellish hound bit and scratched in a frenzy from the outside. Like the big bad wolf in the story of the three little pigs, Black Shuck tried everything to get in and even jumped onto the flat roof, tearing at it with his huge teeth.

Several hours later, the poor couple's torment ended, and they ventured outside. They naturally expected to find the wooden house covered in scratch and bite marks, but there was no sign of any attack—not even a single paw mark in the damp soil surrounding their home. They moved shortly afterward.

The Shaggy Donkey Story

Around the city of Leeds, in northern England, there have been reports of a dreadful shaggy donkey with huge eyes like red saucers. The natives call the beast Padfoot and swear that it only runs on three legs. To see it is not very good, as it's supposed to indicate that death is not far around the corner.

Bull, Book, and Candle

The wall of Hyssington Church in the town of Bagbury has a huge crack from top to bottom. It was caused by a ghastly phantom bull that was supposed to be the ghost of an evil parishioner—name unknown. Apparently this bull terrorized the neighborhood, eventually causing a posse of twelve local parsons to chase it around the churchyard with bell, book, and candle (a traditional method of excluding people from all things religious). The bull apparently disappeared as it charged into the wall and was never seen again.

The Ghostly Pigeon

I've never liked pigeons much—nasty flappy things that poop everywhere. Flying rats I calls 'em. There was once a famous Australian opera singer, however, called Dame Nellie Melba, who became well-known for her pet white pigeon (and a dessert called peach melba).

Except it wasn't really! The bird was no more than a ghost, and nobody else ever saw it. The ghost followed her everywhere, supposedly bringing her good luck. It became so much a part of her life that, in the end, she wouldn't go on stage unless she could actually see it fluttering about.

Monkey Business

There was a Polish medium called Franck Kluski who produced some weird apparitions at his séances (meetings to contact the dead). Between 1913 and 1923, he became famous for producing animals and birds, and nobody has ever been able to explain how he did it (or why, come to think of it). He even arranged for photographs to be taken to prove their existence.

The first was a huge hawklike bird that scared the wits out of the other sitters by flying around the room smashing everything and everyone with its wings, before settling on old Kluski's shoulders. Next was a small, weaselly thing that scampered across the table and sniffed the hands and faces of the astonished sitters with its cold little nose. Just as they were recovering, Kluski produced a huge black dog with massive fangs and glowing eyes, usually accompanied by an old man who stopped it from biting everyone.

But all of this was nothing compared to his final offering. It took the form of a huge shaggy half-ape, half-human, which, though relatively friendly, would think it a great joke to lift up the sofas and bookcases over his head, and even the heaviest members of the audience in their chairs. He was last seen in 1922.

Other mediums have produced seals, cats, and one even managed a phantom pig.

Ghost Pork

Talking of pigs, there is a strange story of a haunting by a whole herd of porkers who lived in south central England. A farmer, called Mr. Brown, when a lad, lived in a small house called Moat Grange. The house stood at the crossing of four roads, which was a traditional site for hanging criminals. One night the Brown family (that's Mr. Brown, Mrs. Brown, and all the little Brownies) was woken by the most terrible commotion. Looking over at the crossroads, they saw a whole load of spooky spotty things that looked like pigs, fighting and tearing up the ground where all the bad people had been buried. The horrified family then had to witness a horrible white face that pressed itself against the window and stared at them.

The ghostly porksters eventually stopped what they were doing and rushed down the road into the darkness. Shortly after, the Brown family left the farm, realizing it was haunted. The pigs were thought at first to be the ghosts of the executed criminals. Later ghost-hunters reckon they were probably just the ghosts of ordinary pigs who felt some sympathy with the ex-criminals.

Here Kitty!

Cats—especially black ones—have always been associated with witches and spells. Before we get into ghost cats, let me tell you of some of the silly superstitions connected with them.

1. If a cat is seen washing its face, expect rain.
2. If ever a cat is seen frolicking on the deck of a ship, it's time to batten down the hatches, as a storm is probably on its way.
3. If an ember jumps from the fire onto your cat, expect an earthquake immediately.
4. In Normandy, France, it is still believed that if you see a tortoiseshell cat climbing a tree, you can confidently expect to be killed in an accident.
5. If a black cat crosses your path in the moonlight, you'll probably suffer a grim death from an epidemic.
6. If two black cats cross your path between 4 and 7 a.m. you can expect to be dead before the day's out.
7. If a strange white cat mews on your doorstep, you must prepare to get married.

Cats were also used as cures in ancient times. French sorcerers liked sprinkling the blood drawn from the vein located under a poor cat's tail to cure skin complaints (how embarrassing). If you were blind, they'd blow the ashes of a roasted cat's head (black) into your eyes three times a day. Which brings us back to ghosts. The inhabitants of the Hebrides (a group of little islands off the western coast of Scotland), right up to 1750, believed that cats had amazing occult properties. Best of all was "second sight," the ability to see beyond what us mere mortals see. (You often get that feeling when you see a cat staring wide-eyed into empty space.) To get yourself in touch with the workings of a cat's mind, they reckoned you had to sacrifice as many black cats as you could get your hands on. This is how they did it (cat lovers, please leave now).

First they fastened a black cat to a spit and roasted it slowly over a low fire. As soon as the poor puss was done, they cooked another, and then another without stopping. Eventually the poor cats' caterwauling became so continuous and loud that it summoned up a horde of ghost cats who joined in the chorus. When the noise reached pandemonium level, a massive spectral cat would suddenly appear. This cat, who apparently spoke perfect English (or Scottish), promised the guy doing all the roasting any wish . . . provided he stopped what he was doing. Nine times out of ten, the cat roaster would ask for the gift of second sight, which was highly sought after in the Hebrides (and a bunch of new cats, I'd have thought?).

The Cat and the Baboon

Now here's a weird one to finish. In 1840 a Mr. Bishop bought a house called Swallows on a two-acre plot in a small village in southern England. He'd only been there a couple of weeks when two of his servants resigned, claiming that the place was haunted by a large cat and a baboon (odd, I'd have thought). If that wasn't bad enough, they swore they'd heard screams coming from the attic and the groans of people being strangled and tortured from the cellar under the dairy. The news spread through the village like wildfire, and people came from far and wide to see for themselves. Several villagers claimed to have seen the cat and the baboon coming from the grating of the dairy cellar.

By this time, old Mr. Bishop had had enough and decided to get rid of the house. He managed somehow to sell it to a mad old colonel in 1842, but the poor old guy lasted even less time. Trying to sell a house with resident ghosts is practically impossible, so it was torn down to make room for a row of cottages. The trouble with ghosts is that, once in, they refuse to move, and these were no exception. Nobody would live in these cottages, so they were torn down shortly after they were built, forming the first haunted rental plots.

So who and what were these ghosts? The most popular story is that Swallows was occupied by a famous highwayman called Steeplechase Jock (his dad was a Scottish chieftain) who plied his trade in the area and buried his victims around the premises. He was said to have had an unpleasant end—turning completely mad and throwing himself into a vat of boiling tar. The ape and the cat were supposed to be the ghosts of poor Jock and his horse, though heaven knows why (or which was which).

NICE TO SEE YOU—AGAIN

Ever since time began, people have tried their level best to get in touch with their ex-nearest and dearest. The quickest and safest way is through a movement called spiritualism.

Born in New York

In 1847, in the small American town of Hydesville, the Fox family heard rapping all night (and it wasn't from next door's stereo). Mrs. Fox apparently asked the noise if it was a spirit and if so to knock twice. Two ear-splitting bangs followed. Mrs. Fox then communicated with the "spirit" through a series of raps until she found out (heaven knows how) that the knocker was the ghost of a peddler who'd been murdered by the last tenant and buried in the basement. The person in question denied it emphatically, but over fifty years later, a false wall was discovered and behind it a pile of human bones.

This didn't help the poor Fox family. By that time, the raps had turned into bloodcurdling groans, and there were sounds that were remarkably like a body being dragged across the floor. It all caused poor Ma Fox's hair to turn white. Eventually the spirit let it be known that "the truth" must be proclaimed to the world, and, from nowhere, hundreds of newfangled mediums found out that they could talk to the spirits. This all culminated in the birth of the spiritualist movement, which was launched in the Corinthian Hall, New York, in 1849. Within a couple of years, it had swept across the Christian world.

Mediums Not Rare

Nowadays spiritualist mediums are everywhere—there's probably one within a few streets of where you live. These odd people claim to be able to get in touch with the spirits of the dead and even make a living from it. If you suddenly want to have a word with your ex-Great Auntie Nellie, for instance, you could do worse than visit your local medium and ask the person to call her up for you. Usually there'll be a few other people at this séance, all wanting a brief word with their dear departed.

The idea is that you all sit in a circle holding hands in the dark, while the medium goes into a sort of a trance. Then he or she asks if there's anyone out there. Well, not just anybody, only spirits connected in some way with those in the room. Suddenly, if you're lucky, you hear your Great Auntie Nellie speaking through the medium, and you can talk to her.

"Hello, Auntie Nellie, are you having a nice time in heaven?"

"I would be if you folks wouldn't keep disturbing me. Why can't you leave me in peace?"

"Sorry, you miserable old bag, I thought you might not be quite so grumpy up there."

This is how séances usually go, but lots of these mediums have been found to have elaborate tricks up their sleeves to fool people like you and me. Tape recorders behind curtains, people moaning from other rooms,

or even the weird white stuff that appears to come from their mouths called ectoplasm. This stuff is supposed to be a substance halfway between the spirit world and the one we live in.

Do-It-Yourself Séances

There used to be a sort of game that you could actually buy in Victorian shops called Ouija (from the French word for "yes"). It was all the rage in the pre-television late-nineteenth century, either as a fun game for the whole family or to be used in a séance.

The Ouija board was an oblong piece of wood with all the letters of the alphabet written around its edge in a half moon shape. On top of this was placed a much smaller, heart-shaped board mounted on tiny castors. Each person would then put his or her index finger on the heart-shaped board, and it would move around spelling out answers to questions. Unfortunately, many people didn't really know what they were getting into, and there were horrendous stories of the "players" being scared out of their wits. Certainly not to be tried at home.

Painting by Memory

The twentieth-century painter L. S. Lowry was a rent collector by day and in the evenings painted little matchstick men in the industrial town of Salford in northern England. Another painter called William Turner managed to get the famous old man to sit for the one and only oil painting ever to be done of him. Unfortunately, Turner was on the slow side, so much so that poor old Lowry died mid-painting, and Turner had to finish it from memory.

Just as he was about to sell the painting in 1993, a well-known medium claimed he'd been visited by the very dead

Lowry. While chatting, the old ghost had mentioned not only that he was still doing a few drawings but also that he liked the painting that Turner had done of him. He then went on to say that the work should be sold in aid of a local charity (run by the medium no doubt). Poor old Turner had to abide by his wishes.

Lots of famous people are supposed to have come back through mediums, including John Lennon, Marilyn Monroe, and George Orwell. Even the infamous Jesse James turned up saying he hadn't really meant to shoot all those people. Who would you like to talk to if you could bring them back? (I'd like to give that Mr. Hitler a piece of my mind.)

SORRY FOLKS

GHOST HORSE

Poltergeists

Poltergeists are like ghosts you can't actually see. The word *poltergeist* is of German origin and means "noisy spirit." Poltergeists have a bad reputation, but not all poltergeists are nasty, and some even seem to have a sense of humor. Although many become infamous for throwing furniture around and generally making a terrible mess, there are reports of some that have actually been known to break in just to clean up. We could all do with one of them!

If one of the main differences between poltergeists and ghosts is that the former can't be seen, the other is that they tend not to hang around one place for very long. Sometimes poltergeists disappear in a matter of weeks. Others get attached to a particular person rather than a place and follow him or her around. Poltergeists have hardly ever done anyone any physical harm, tending to act more like misbehaving schoolboys.

Pandemonium at Number 50
The address was the very fashionable Berkeley Square in London, and the year was 1840. Although number 50 was

empty of furniture, neighbors began to hear the sounds of huge articles being dragged across the upstairs floors. Also the bells used for summoning servants would resound throughout the deserted house in the middle of the night. When investigators entered, all they found were the bells swinging—no further sound was heard.

Worse was still to come. At the peak of the activity, several windows were flung open by invisible hands, and stones, books, and even old shoes were flung into the street below. Finally, one morning, passersby noticed that every window in the house had been smashed.

Why this house in particular? The story goes that long before this all happened, a mad member of a very aristocratic family was held in one of the rooms and fed through a slit in the door. After he died, there were several reports that the room held a pulsating mass of evil-smelling, panting matter with dozens of little red eyes.

Well, when a young man-about-town, Sir Robert Warboys, heard about the strange goings-on at Number 50, he accepted a challenge to sleep there overnight. He didn't believe a word of the stories but was made to take a gun with him just in case. His pals also insisted that they stand guard downstairs from the dreaded room where Sir Robert was to stay.

Poor Robert had only been in the room for only about forty-five minutes when his friends heard the blast of a single gunshot. When they reached the room, they found their friend slumped across the bed—dead. But he hadn't been shot. His expression told all—eyes wide open and lips curled hideously over his clenched teeth. He had simply died of fright.

The house stood empty for years (are you surprised?), but on Christmas Eve 1887, two slightly drunken sailors, knowing

nothing of its reputation and having just docked in London, broke in for somewhere to stay for the night. They woke up to a shapeless mass moving around the house. Terrified, one of them, Robert Martin, managed to flee the house to get help. When he returned with a policeman, they found his friend Edward Blunden on the ground with his face in the most horrible grimace. His neck had been snapped like a twig.

If you are completely bonkers and want to visit the house, it's still there, and the last I heard it was a bookshop.

The Painting Poltergeist

Matthew Manning achieved fame at the tender age of fifteen when he became a psychic. Unfortunately, it all went downhill when in 1970 a poltergeist decided to concentrate on his family's 200-year-old house. This particular poltergeist became famous throughout the world for his crazy stunts like bending cutlery and painting frenzied pictures in the style of famous old masters. (Why complain? You could probably

make quite a profit, I'd have thought.) Manning, by the way, turned from stylish party tricks to spiritual healing, which made him even more famous.

Hair Today Gone Tomorrow

In 1837 poltergeists turned up in Menomonie, Wisconsin. A poor little girl was standing with her mother when, out of the blue, huge chunks of her hair simply disappeared into thin air leaving her practically bald. In another instance, in 1969, one of Bishop James Pike's assistants awoke to find her hair singed off in a straight line. This happened again and again until three weeks later when some of the locks appeared on her pillow beside her. The bishop put it down to his son's recent suicide.

Better the Devil You Know

Here's a bizarre one. In 1889 a farmer named George Dagg, who lived in Quebec province, Canada, noticed weird things happening around the milking parlor. Milk pans were overturned, windows were smashed, and small fires were cropping up everywhere. The focus for all this stuff was a small orphaned girl named Dinah McLean, who was often found screaming after the poltergeist had attacked her. At first she was the only person who could hear it, but later it muttered very obnoxious things to Mr. Dagg in a low, gruff voice and then claimed it was the devil.

It finally agreed to leave and, on the day in question, hordes of villagers turned up to hear it, through George, supplying personal and somewhat embarrassing information about them. Then it claimed it wasn't a devil after all, but an angel sent by God (a very odd foul-mouthed angel at that). The following day some village children swore they'd watched a "beautiful man in white" rising into the sky.

THINGS THAT GO BUMP
IN THE NIGHT

Many things that happen can't necessarily be explained by the term ghosts. We've all heard bumpings and creakings in the night and have all seen scary faces in everyday objects when we're not even trying. Here are a few of the oddest things.

Light Fantastic

Some of the most common sightings are lights that either fly through the air, race across a room, or just hover in the sky. These can be interpreted as fairies, UFOs, will-o'-the-wisps, or whatever, but there's usually a perfectly good explanation.

Some scientists have described a commonly seen phenomenon as "floating ball" lightning and claim it's perfectly harmless. But an inquisitive child was reported in 1943 to have kicked out at one, and the resulting explosion killed him and eleven unfortunate cows who happened to be standing nearby.

In Wales they call these floating lights "corpse candles," and they are said to predict imminent death. On one occasion, a whole busload of passengers traveling in southern Wales spotted three pale lights hovering over a river. The next day, three men were drowned when their boat capsized at exactly the same spot.

Old Red Eye

In 1965 a moving light chased and caught a man called Terry Pell who was driving his vegetable truck in southern England. The light was like a huge red eye and stuck itself to his windshield. Mr. Pell's wife and daughter, who'd been asleep at his side, woke up and were terrified at the apparition. It then detached itself and soared off into the distance.

Forty-five minutes earlier, Mrs. Rachel Atwill noticed a bright light in the sky accompanied by a horrible droning noise that lasted twenty-five minutes. It gave poor Mrs. Atwill a headache, and she was forced to have a large brandy to calm herself down. (Maybe she had the large brandy before seeing the light and hearing the noise.)

Glow Toe

If you think that's spooky, what about the American woman who noticed, just as she was going to bed, that the fourth toe on her right foot was glowing. When she rubbed it, the light spread up her foot and began to smell. Her husband told her to wash her foot (I'm not surprised), but it had no effect. The light eventually disappeared after about forty-five minutes, never to return.

Beware the Invisibles

In some places, ghosts are called invisibles. In 1761 in northern Italy, five farmwomen were returning from the woods where they'd been collecting sticks for the fire. Without any warning, one of them screamed and fell to the ground as cold as yesterday's pasta.

When her friends came near, they were sickened by what they saw. Her clothes were finely shredded and thrown all around her up to six feet away. A huge wound on her head exposed her skull, and her stomach had been ripped open exposing her intestines. If that wasn't bad enough, most of the flesh from one thigh had been removed and her femur pulled from its socket. Doctors examining the body found no sign of blood and said she looked just like the victim of an explosion.

Poor Little Harry

One poor boy had obviously upset one of these invisibles. In 1850 Dr. Phelps's young son, Harry, became the victim of a terrible series of attacks. As he walked down the street, stones were thrown at him from nowhere, and at home he would sometimes be lifted so high from his chair that his head would bang on the ceiling. Imagine that when you're having dinner!

WILL YOU PLEASE SIT DOWN

Once, in front of a large group of people, he was lifted right up into a tree, and his clothes were shredded before the poor boy was tossed into a water tank.

Poor Little Eleonore

Lastly—if you're still not convinced—in a pamphlet written in 1850, there was a description of a series of attacks on children. One little girl, called Eleonore Zugum, was seen to be throttled by an invisible hand that pressed in the sides of her neck. Later on, other children were jerked around and even spat on. Witnesses then watched in horror as the children were bitten more than twenty times on their arms, leaving teeth marks and rings of foul-smelling spit in the shape of mouths.

VAMPIRES

Lots of people don't believe in ghosts—but they do believe in vampires. Vampires are dead people who leave their graves at night to suck the blood of the living—for a living. Here are a few for you to mull over.

Peter Plogojowitz

This well-known vampire apparently lived in the village of Kisilova in Hungary in the eighteenth century. After terrorizing the poor villagers for six weeks after his death, they opened his grave and found him still dead but actually looking better than ever. His skin was pink, and his nails and hair had grown. His mouth, however, was full of fresh blood from his victims, which revealed what he was. The villagers then whipped old Peter out of the coffin and burned him to a cinder, which seemed to do the trick nicely.

Strangers in the Night

This strange story comes from a tribunal in Belgrade, Serbia. Government officials, along with a doctor, traveled to a certain village following the tale of a soldier who'd been invited to dinner by a pleasant farmer and his family. While eating, so the story goes, a complete stranger came into the room and joined them (odd!). Everyone seemed frightened, apart from the soldier who kept quiet out of politeness. The next day the farmer was dead, and a couple of the others spoke up and said the mysterious guest had been the farmer's grandfather who'd passed away over ten years before. The old boy had been suspected of being a vampire for ages. When they investigated the old stiff's tomb, he, too, was in perfect shape. When they opened a vein, fresh blood squirted out. (I hope you're not eating while reading this.) Anyway, they chopped off the old guy's head, hoping that would do it, but at that point several people came forward and claimed that

he'd been a member of a sort of local vampire club. They then opened four more graves only to find the inhabitants also looking absolutely healthy (for dead people!). They were all nailed into their coffins and burned.

Arnold Paul of Madreiga

Arnold Paul lived on the Turkish-Serbian border in the eighteenth century. He was well known in his village because he was always moaning about being pestered by an old Turkish vampire. (Who could blame him for that?) Poor Arnold was killed one day when a hay cart fell on him. Luckily, before he died he'd managed to dine on some earth from the said vampire's grave, which apparently was a well-known way to keep the inhabitant quiet.

Unfortunately, it didn't work, and old Arnold turned into a bigger and better (or worse) vampire than the Turk had ever been. When in 1730 they opened Arnold's coffin, he was covered in blood that was bubbling out of his veins. The local police ordered that his heart be pierced, but when it was done, Arnold screamed at the top of his lungs. Some people never learn.

Vampire Calling

Here's a good one. A vampire from a village in Bohemia used to call his victims to him and then have his way with them. Eventually the villagers got wise to this and, opening his grave, tied him to a post stuck firmly in the earth.

"How friendly you are," the corpse said in a deep voice, "to give me a stick with which I can drive away the dogs." Nice to find a vampire with a sense of humor, I think.

Anyway, they'd hardly left before he'd risen again and suffocated five people. The next day, the local hangman dug him up and, using a metal spike, filled him with holes. They then carried him to a huge fire, but as they walked, he howled at the top of his lungs and thrashed his arms and legs.

Vampire Viewing

Do you want to see a real live vampire? (Or should I say a real dead vampire?) You can, so I'm told, if you dare hang around probably the spookiest and most fabulous graveyard in England at night. Highgate Cemetery in north London has 45,000 graves, and the whole place reeks of ruin and decay, with overgrown catacombs and vaults everywhere you look. It's a dead certainty for ghosts and vampires. All this, and it's open to the public—amazing!

There are reports galore of ghostly goings-on, none more scary than the one about a terrifying old woman, with long white hair, who glides among the scary tombs and in and out of the moldering vaults. She's thought to be the ghost of a madwoman who in younger life murdered her own two kids, before starting on a long career as a vampire. She now tours the vast cemetery forever searching for the graves of those whose blood she'd sucked. Something to do for an evening, I suppose.

Getting Rid of Unwanted Vampires

Vampires, as you can imagine, can be a real nuisance. If you are currently troubled by them, there's a simple kit you can put together to keep the creepy things at bay. First, you'll need to know if the person you suspect is one *is* one. This is quite simple. Take a normal hand mirror and hold it up to him or her. If you can't see their reflection, then you could be in trouble.

To keep him or her at bay, you could wear a string of garlic around your neck (it'll probably keep everyone else at bay too) or wave a silver cross at them. (If you suspect they might be werewolves, shoot 'em with a silver bullet.) Failing that, and if you know which grave they live in, you could do far worse than the old stake-through-the-heart routine, which is practically guaranteed to finish 'em off.

WHERE'VE I GONE?

GHOST HUNTING AND WHAT TO DO IF YOU SEE ONE

Going out especially to look for ghosts is pretty pointless. Just like buses, they're never there when you want them.

More Than Meets the Eye

People still try to find ghosts, however, and every year some new gizmo or other is brought out to try and fool ghosts into revealing themselves. Forget tape recorders and thermometers, they're very old hat. Nowadays your average ghostbuster uses elaborate see-in-the-dark video cameras, which they let run all night. One of these is called the Spider and was developed by a famous ghost hunter named Tony Cornell.

Most investigators simply go to believe-to-be-haunted places, set up all their cameras, microphones, tripwires, and other gadgets, and then sit back and wait—and wait. It's kind of like fishing . . . only without any bait. Nothing of any real interest has come forward from these investigations. This either means that ghosts are camera shy, or that they need an actual real live human in the room, or that they really are only in the imagination of the onlooker. Most real scientists don't believe in ghosts, therefore, because there's no scientific way of studying them.

Ghost Tricksters

There are some weirdos, however, who take it much farther. They get so caught up in the whole ghastly ghostly business that they form ghost clubs, running off for long weekends to seek ghosts. These people hang around old houses and spooky places with special equipment in order to try and trick the ghosts into revealing themselves. The trouble is, just like the people who go out looking for UFOs, some of them fiddle around with the evidence, for reasons best known to themselves, just to fool us.

Ghostly Ways

If you are still determined to try ghost hunting, there are a few things you might need to know.

According to the experts, most ghosts are a pretty aimless bunch, simply drifting around with no real purpose. Having said that, if the ghost in question belongs to a relative or friend, they often try to make contact. Usually the ghosts don't seem to know or care if real people are around. They tend to stick to houses rather than humans.

Ghosts aren't much good at conversation. If they do talk, they tend to get it over with quickly. And because they're not actually made of anything, they tend to be pretty harmless. Therefore, most people will survive being punched by a ghost . . . unless they die of fright. We live people are only really scared of them because we don't know what they are.

Some ghosts, however, can cause physical grief, like in the story of the vicar's wife who was rescued by one ghost from being throttled by another (a monk ghost, as it happens). She carried real live bruises on her neck for ages.

What to Do If You See a Ghost

If you go out hunting with a group of friends and you happen to end up in the presence of a ghost, only one of you will see it. If you do happen to be the chosen one, this is what you should do.

1. Keep completely still. Don't move a muscle—you might frighten it away.
2. If the ghost speaks to you, be very polite. Ask it its name and age, what sex it is (if you can't tell), and what it's come back for (to see old friends, scare the life out of someone, etc.).

3. Ask if it's in any sort of trouble, and, if it is, see if there's anything you can do to help.
4. Invite the ghost to come back again, but make sure you get it to say what time and where it will be arriving, otherwise you could be standing around in the dark forever.
5. Wait until the ghost moves before you do. If it leaves through an open door, try following. But if the door's

closed, take care not to injure yourself. If at all possible, go around to see what's on the other side.

Ghost Busters

If you have a bad ghost you want to get rid of, you will find that most church officials perform services called exorcisms. Apparently you only have to call the local church, and they'll send someone over to flush 'em out—like unplugging blocked pipes—except ghost removal's free!

Home Exorcism in Ten Easy Steps

(By the way, make sure the person doing the exorcism has no yucky habits or dark secrets, otherwise the evil spirit might jump across to him.)

1. Do it somewhere where there's a connection between the demon and the victim—like a bedroom.

2. Gather together some salt (representing purity), red wine (representing the blood of Jesus), and a bucket of holy water.

3. Give the victim a cross to hold and maybe some bones of a saint (if you happen to have any in the house).

4. Try to find out the identity of the actual demon. It is most important.

5. Recite as many biblical scriptures and prayers as you can think of.

6. Beware! When the demon finally gives in, be prepared for pandemonium and lots of foul language and even worse smells. The demon usually turns on the victim and abuses him, using the victim's own voice.

7. Silence the demon's voice in order to continue.

8. As his voice dies out, one may feel a spiritual and physical pressure. The demon has collided with the "will of the kingdom" and is in direct conflict with the exorcist.

9. The demon is now looking for somewhere to go. It most certainly doesn't want to go home to hell, however.

10. In a triumph of God's will, the exorcist dismisses the spirit in the name of Jesus. Everyone present feels great relief.

11. Nobody present should have any secret sins, for, as the demon leaves, it'll shout them out for all to hear and probably ruin the exorcism.

The Bitter End

Just in case you're in any way tempted to throw a sheet over your head just before bedtime and scare your brother or sister half to death, take heed of this little story.

Erasmus, a Dutchman and scholar of Greek, tells of a very rich and good-looking lady who witnessed a ghost in her bedchamber. Instead of running, she grabbed a big stick and beat the living daylights out of what turned out to be a man hiding under a sheet trying to scare her—"until he screamed out for mercy."

Well, I hope you've now got a better picture of ghosts after reading this book, although I'm not sure whether you'll believe in them more now that you've reached the end, or less. Personally, the only way I'd really believe in ghosts is if I met one myself. So far I haven't, but I've come pretty close. Many years ago, I revisited a small hotel on a cliffside in southwestern England that I'd once stayed at. It was locked up and deserted. I left my girlfriend at the front, while I had a look around. As I was strolling back, I could hear her talking. I asked her whom she'd met, and she was surprised that I hadn't seen the couple of old ladies who'd told her they were the owners. There was no sign of them, and you could see for miles around.

That evening, in the local bar, we learned that a year ago the two sisters who had run the place had tragically died within two months of each other and the hotel was up for sale.

Anyway, that's the end of my little history of ghosts. Although, when pressed, I'm still not sure they really exist, nothing in the world could persuade me to spend the night in a lonely graveyard. How about you?

By the way, what's that dark shape looming just behind you?

GHOST SPEAK

afreet: an Arabic word referring to powerful evil spirits (created from the death of a murdered man) that are out for revenge

afterlife: life after life, or actually, after death

alû: known for occupying deserted places in ancient Mesopotamia and squeezing their victims to death—like a boa constrictor. These ghosts looked like humans except for the many missing body parts.

astral light: a substance or energy field that supposedly forms images from thought. Also called Akasha.

Bauta: a little red-bodied, big-headed Indian ghost that accepts edible bribery

Bhut: a cranky spirit that pesters the living because its person suffered a wrongful death or received an inadequate burial. The nerve! To avoid them, Indian lore suggests lying flat on the ground.

demon: a ghost, yes, but an evil one that spreads agony and devastation

ectoplasm: a visible substance that appears when a spirit materializes through the body of a medium (the goo usually spills out of the medium's mouth—ick)

exorcism: the act of getting rid of an evil spirit by reciting special prayers and using tools—crosses, potions, school lunches—to scare it away

hellhound: a canine guardian of the underworld as depicted in mythology—not your average domestic pooch

highwayman: a roadside thief that attacked travelers in eighteenth-century England. Sneaky plug: read my book about highwaymen to learn more.

khu: one of six parts in every person, according to ancient Egyptian thought. This spirit felt lonely when its person—and the other five parts—died and would cause problems for the living out of jealousy and boredom.

medium: a person through whom the world of people and the world of spirits can communicate. So much for the telephone and the Internet!

mummy: a dead body that has been preserved with special salts and resins and wrapped in cloth to make it last for a very long time. But that's not the scary part. The scary part is when those mummies come back to life in the movies.

Obeah: a belief in harnessing supernatural forces through magic, sorcery, witchcraft, etc., for one's personal use. Brought and developed by slaves from Africa, Obeah exists in and around the Caribbean (mainly the West Indies, South America, and the southern United States). The practice has many names in the islands, including Shango, Santeria, voodoo, and Ju-Ju.

occult: matters involving secret skills or powers that can control the supernatural world

Ouija: a tool, often sold as a board game, used to solicit messages from the spirit world

phantom: a ghost that exists in shadowy appearance only

poltergeist: an active ghost that can't be seen but makes itself known by making noise and messes

reincarnation: a spirit's receipt of a new body after death

Saint Elmo's Fire: a fiery phenomenon that appears around airplanes or ships, usually in storms

séance: a meeting that aims to receive communication from the spirits of dead people

sorcerer: someone who performs magic by controlling evil spirits; a wizard

specter: a visible ghost

spirtualist: a person who believes that humans can communicate with spirits

trance: an unconscious or semiconscious state brought on by hypnosis, the shock of seeing a ghost, etc.

vampire: like Dracula, an alive dead-person who comes from the grave and wants to suck your blood

voodoo: a religion based on the belief in magic, charms, and ancestor worship that began in Africa and is still practiced in some parts of the West Indies

zombie: a supernaturally reanimated dead person or automaton. Or me, after staying up all night to finish this book.

FURTHER READING

Allan, Tony. *Tales of Real Haunting.* Tulsa, OK: EDC Publishing, 1997.

Alphin, Elaine Marie. *Ghost Soldier.* New York: Henry Holt and Company, 2001.

Blackwood, Gary L. *Spooky Spectres.* New York: Benchmark Books, 2000.

Cohen, Daniel. *Dangerous Ghosts.* New York: G. P. Putnam's Sons, 1996.

Crowe, Carole. *Sharp Horns on the Moon.* Honesdale, PA: Boyds Mills Press, 1998.

Downer, Deborah A. *Classic American Ghost Stories.* Little Rock, AR: August House Publishers, 1990.

Ibbotson, Eva. *Dial-A-Ghost.* New York: Dutton Books, 2001.

Landau, Elaine. *Ghosts.* Brookfield, CT: Millbrook Press, 1995.

Maynard, Christopher. *Ghosts.* Cambridge, MA: Candlewick Press, 1999.

McKissack, Pat. *The Dark-Thirty: Southern Tales of the Supernatural.* New York: Knopf, 1992.

Netzley, Patricia D. *Haunted Houses.* San Diego, CA: Lucent Books, 2000.

San Souci, Robert D. *Short and Shivery: Thirty Creepy Tales.* New York: Yearling, 2001.

Vande Velde, Vivian. *Being Dead: Stories.* San Diego: Harcourt, 2001.

WEBSITES

The American Ghost Society
   <http://www.prairieghosts.com/>
Castle of Spirits
   <http://www.castleofspirits.com/>
Eeeek-NET!™
   <http://www.eeeek.com>
The Ghost Club
   <http://www.ghostclub.org.uk/>
Ghost Research Society
   <http://www.ghostresearch.org/>
Haunted Places Directory
   <http://www.haunted-places.com/>
International Ghost Hunters Society
   <http://www.ghostweb.com/>
Museum of Talking Boards
   <http://www.museumoftalkingboards.com/>
National Ghost Hunters Society
   <http://www.nationalghosthunters.com/kids.html>
Obiwan's UFO-Free Paranormal Page
   <http://www.ghosts.org/>
The Shadowlands
   <http://www.theshadowlands.net/>
Shadowmag
   <http://www.shadowmag.com/>

INDEX

Abershaw, Jerry, 29
afreets, 19
Akasha, 12
alû, 15
American ghosts, 47–48, 64, 71, 74
ancient Roman ghosts, 21
animal ghosts, 55–63
Argyll, duke of, 50
Assyrian ghosts, 15
Athenodouros, 21
Australia, 44, 52

Bacon, Sir Francis, 56
Bautas, 14
Bell, John, 47–48
Bhuts, 14
Bisham Abbey, 45
black cats, 61–62, 63
Black Shuck, 57
Bohemia, 79
British country ghosts, 37–43
British Museum, 18, 19
Brome, Theophilus, 49
Bruce, Sir Michael, 54
Brutus, 21

Cairo, 16, 17, 19
Caribbean ghosts, 23
Carnarvon, Lord George, 16
Chinese ghosts, 21–22

Christianity, 9, 50
Covent Garden, 30, 33, 34
Crusades, 19
Cumberland, duke of, 30

Duffy, Barney, 44

ectoplasm, 11
Egyptian ghosts, 16–19
Elizabeth I, Queen, 45, 46
Emery, Walter, 16
England, 17, 19, 20, 37, 38, 41, 42, 49, 50, 54, 58, 60, 62, 66, 74, 80, 87
England, Bank of, 31–32
Ewloe Castle, 41

ghost cities, 50
ghostly behavior, 10–11, 14–27, 29–30, 32–43, 45, 47–48, 51, 56–57, 59, 63–72, 74–75, 80, 83, 87
ghosts, 7–87; of America, 64, 47–48, 71; ancient, 14–15, 16, 21, 23; around the world, 13–23; of Assyria, 15; behavior of, 10–11, 14–27, 29–30, 32–43, 45, 47–48, 51, 56–57, 59, 63–72, 74–75, 80, 83, 87; of Britain, 24–43, 61, 73; busting of, 22, 85–86; of Canada, 72;

95

of the Caribbean, 23; of China, 21–22; definition of, 7; of Egypt, 16–19; hunting of, 82–87; of India, 14–15; of London, 18, 24, 28–36, 55, 69, 70; modern, 24–27; theories about, 10, 12
ghost ships, 50, 51, 52
ghost stories, 44–48
Glamis Castle, 40
Goddard, Sir Victor, 24
gods and goddesses, 16, 23, 9, 14
graveyards, 11, 29–30, 32, 37, 49, 77, 78, 79, 80

Haiti, 23
hauntings, 9, 35, 52, 63
hellhounds, 57
highwaymen, 29, 63
Hoby, Dame Elizabeth, 45–46
Hungary, 77

Imhotep, 16
Indian ghosts, 14–15
Ireland, 46–47
Islam, 19
Italy, 74

Jackson, Freddie, 24
Jack the Ripper, 32–33
Jamaica, 23

Johnson, Samuel, 10
Julius Caesar, 21

Kluski, Franck, 59

Lacock, Abbess of, 19
life after death, 9
London, 18, 24, 28–36, 55, 69, 70
Longespee, William, 19

Mary I, Queen, 29
mediums, 9, 11, 67, 26, 59, 60, 64–65
Melba, Dame Nellie, 58
mummies, 16, 17, 18
Murray, Douglas, 17–18

Nanking, 22
New York, 19

Obeah, 23
occultists, 10–11
Osiris, 16
Ouija boards, 66

Paul, Arnold, 79
Pliny, 21
poltergeists, 67–68, 70, 71, 72

reincarnation, 12
religion, 9, 14, 16, 19, 23, 29, 50, 72
Roose, 28
Royal Air Force, 24, 43, 54

Saint Elmo's Fire, 52
Saint James Palace, 30–31
samurai, 23
Scotland, 26, 40, 50, 61
séances, 59, 65, 66
Serbia, 77–78
Shakti, 14
Shanghai, 22
Shiva, 14
singing ghosts, 41
Smithfield market, 28–29
South Africa, 51
spiritualists and spirtualism, 9, 23, 64
Stokes, Doris, 26

Tennessee, 47–48

Titanic, 19
Turner, William, 66–67
Tutankhamen, 16

UFOs, 73, 85
unexplained phenomena, 73–76

vampires, 19, 77–81; busting of, 19, 81; definition of, 77
voodoo, 23

Wales, 41, 73
West Africa, 23
Whitehead, Sarah, 31–32
World War I, 24
World War II, 57

zombies, 23

ABOUT THE AUTHOR

John Farman has worked as a commercial illustrator and a cartoonist and has written more than thirty nonfiction books for children. He lives in London, England.